The Magic School Bus PRESENTS
OCEAN ADVENTURE

Scholastic Inc.

ISBN: 978-0-545-67954-1

All text, illustrations, and compilations © 2014 Scholastic Inc.
Based on the Magic School Bus series © Joanna Cole and Bruce Degen
Text by Mary Kay Carson
Illustrations by Carolyn Bracken

Published by Scholastic Inc., 557 Broadway, New York, NY 10012.

12 11 10 9 8 7 6 5 4 3 2 1   14 15 16 17 18 19/0

Printed in the U.S.A.
First printing, September 2014

Earth is an ocean planet. Almost three-fourths of our world is covered in ocean. From space, the **continents** look like islands.

LET'S DIVE IN AND FIND OUT MORE ABOUT THE OCEAN AND WHAT LIVES THERE, STUDENTS!

DIVE IN? UH-OH...

A **CONTINENT** is a large landmass on Earth. Earth has seven continents. They are Asia, Africa, Europe, North America, South America, Australia, and Antarctica.

An ocean is a huge area of salty water. There are five oceans — the Pacific, Atlantic, Indian, Arctic, and Southern Oceans. The largest ocean is the Pacific.

Earth's continents separate the five oceans. But all ocean waters are connected. They mix together to make one global ocean.

Some of the salt in the ocean comes from land. Rain breaks down rocks over time. Rainwater washes out the salt in rocks as they break down.

IT'S EASIER TO FLOAT IN SALT WATER THAN IN FRESHWATER.

Then the rainwater carries salt into rivers that empty into the sea. All the salt in seawater makes it heavier than freshwater.

Thousands of different plants and animals live in the ocean, from the sunny surface down to the dark seafloor. The ocean is home to the enormous blue whale, jellyfish with deadly stingers, slime that glows in the dark, and sharks with heads shaped like hammers. Coasts and beaches are where land meets sea.

HAMMERHEAD SHARK

JELLYFISH

Animals that live on beaches are underwater at high tide, but must survive without water when the tide goes out. Some cling to rocks while others hide under damp seaweeds or stay in tide pools where it never gets dry.

PHYTOPLANKTON are tiny plants that float freely in water. They need sunlight to grow.

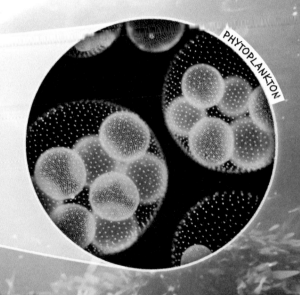

PHYTOPLANKTON

All plants need sunlight to survive. It's how they make food. Ocean plants like sea grass and seaweed live only where there is sunlight. Masses of tiny plants called **phytoplankton** drift near the ocean's surface. They are so small they can be seen only with a microscope.

Some of the brightest areas in the ocean are **coral reefs**. They are sunny, warm, and busy with colorful life.

SEA TURTLE

CLOWNFISH

IS THERE A PEARL IN THERE?

Reefs are piled-up skeletons of **coral** animals. Coral reefs make up a very small part of the sea. However, one-quarter of the ocean's creatures live on coral reefs.

SEA STAR

MORAY EEL

A **CORAL REEF** is made by lots of different corals. Corals are tiny ocean animals related to jellyfish. They have tube-shaped bodies with tentacles. Coral make a shell or skeleton around themselves. New coral animals grow on top of dead ones, building up a reef over time.

Ocean hunters, like sharks, are called **predators**. The animals they kill for food are **prey**. To hide from each other, predators and prey are often **camouflaged**. Many creatures that live in sunny water are colored to blend in. Their skin or scales are darker on top and lighter underneath. It's hard to see something white looking up from below. It disappears into the sunlight. Dark bodies are difficult to spot looking down through water. They fade into the darkness below.

CARPET SHARK

EAGLERA

A **PREDATOR** is an animal that hunts. It catches and eats prey for food.

Dive deeper and the ocean gets darker. Much of the ocean is only dimly lit and some parts are very cold. Enough sunlight gets through to tell day from night. But it's too dark for plants to grow.

Without plants, there are no plant-eating animals. Food is hard to come by. Still, there are some sea creatures that can live there. Creatures live under great pressure, which is caused by the weight of all the water above.

FEEL THAT PRESSURE PUSHING DOWN ON US?

I DON'T DO WELL UNDER PRESSURE!

COELACANTH

CHAMBERED NAUTILUS

COMB JELLIES

Lots of weird fish live in deep parts of the ocean. In the deeper, darker water most are small and are black or brown so they can't be seen. Others, like hatchetfish, live where there is dim light. Their silvery scales reflect the light and help them disappear. Fangtooth fish and viperfish use their big mouths and spiky teeth to gulp down prey.

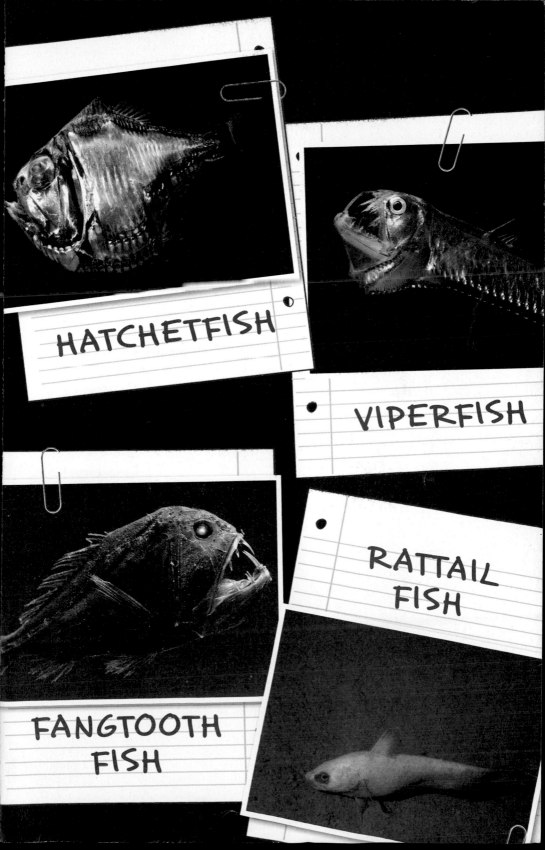

HATCHETFISH

VIPERFISH

RATTAIL
FISH

FANGTOOTH
FISH

ATOLLA
JELLY

FLASHLIGHT
FISH

FIREFLY
SQUID

ANGLERFISH

In the dark of the deep ocean, some animals turn on a light! The ability to make light is called **bioluminescence**.

Some fish, like flashlight fish, use light to communicate. It helps them find mates and stay in groups. An anglerfish uses its light as **bait**. It brings in prey.

BIOLUMINESCENCE ISN'T JUST FOR THE FISH. SOME INSECTS USE IT, TOO.

FIREFLIES HAVE BIOLUMINESCENCE.

DEEP OCEAN

BIOLUMINESCENCE is light that glows from living things. Chemicals inside the animals create the light.

Most of the ocean is completely dark. It's so deep that sunlight never reaches it. There's no difference between day and night in the dark ocean. Temperatures are near freezing and the weight of water makes pressure extreme. It's a hard place to live and find food.

TRIPOD
FISH

SNIPE EEL

HAGFISH

GIANT
OARFISH

In the deep, dark ocean there are hot-water vents on the seafloor. All kinds of strange creatures live near them. There are eyeless shrimp, giant tube worms, and spider crabs. Hot water and volcanic gases flow out of vents on the seafloor. **Bacteria** grow by using these gases. Sea creatures eat the bacteria.

BACTERIA are too small to see without a powerful microscope. They are a type of simple living thing that live nearly everywhere.

GIANT TUBE WORMS

SPIDER CRAB

OFFSHORE OIL PLATFORM

OCEAN FISHI

24

Humans live on land, way above the deep sea. Still, humans need the ocean. We harvest fish, seaweed, and other ocean foods. Oil, gas, and minerals come from the ocean, too. Seas are also watery highways. Traders and travelers have sailed the seas for thousands of years. It's why most of the world's large cities are on coasts.

CARGO SHIP

Even if you've never seen the sea, the ocean affects you. Ocean plants make the air breathable. All life needs healthy seas.

Scientists keep watch over the ocean. They check on the water and sea life. Ocean scientists work to solve pollution problems that harm sea life, such as trash, **sewage**, and oil spills.

SEWAGE is wastewater that comes from sewers and drains, including toilets.

An ocean scientist is called an **oceanographer**. Some study how waves move. Others look for new kinds of sea life. We've explored a small part of the ocean. Only about 5 percent! Future oceanographers will have lots more to explore. What do you think they'll find?

THERE'S MUCH MORE TO DISCOVER OUT HERE, STUDENTS!